PROVERBS important things to know

Proverbs FOR CHILDREN

Written by Carol Greene
Illustrated by Gordon Willman

ARCH Books

ST. LOUIS, MISSOURI

MANUFACTURED IN THE UNITED STATES OF AMERICA

ISBN 0-570-06140-7

Susanna was a princess
in a palace long ago
and more than any other thing,
Susanna liked to *know*.

"What's this? What's that? When, where, and why?"
asked curious Susanna.
Her parents tore their royal hair
and sent for Grandma Hannah.

SPECIAL DELIVERY

Grandma came with forty trunks,
and most were filled with books.
"Susanna has her grandma's brains,"
she said, "though not her looks."

"There's nothing wrong with *knowing,* child,"
she told the little girl.
"In fact, some wise folk even say
that knowledge is a pearl.

"So let's go to the garden now
and you can ask away.
I'll bring my books and we'll see what
the Proverbs have to say."

"Is it better to keep busy?"
asked Susanna. "My friend Saul
just sleeps all night and sleeps all day.
He never works at all."

"Well, Saul should watch an ant, my dear.
She hasn't any master.
But when it comes to working hard,
no human can surpass her.

"She gathers food in summer
and hides it safe away.
She never ends up hungry
on the coldest winter day."
—*Proverbs 6:6-11*

Susanna opened up her purse.
"I have ten coins of gold.
Shall I give some to the needy
or save them till I'm old?"

"Giving makes the heart feel glad
and when you learn to share,
you'll see how much the Lord gives *you.*
He cares for those who care."

—*Proverbs 11:24-26*

Susanna took out seven coins.
"I'll give them to the needy.
I know that I should love the poor.
But why? They look so seedy."

“God made the poor as He made you.
He loves them just the same.
When you love them as He does,
you do honor to His name.”
—*Proverbs 14:31*

Just then Susanna looked around
and saw her mother's maid
kissing the chief baker
deep in the garden shade.

"A tittle-tattler always tells,"
said Grandma with a smile.
"But wise girls can keep secrets
and folks trust them a mile."
—Proverbs 11:13

"I told my friend Rebecca
what ugly shoes she had.
She hit me," said Susanna.
"I think I made her mad."

"Words spoken without thinking
can pierce us like a sword,"
said Grandma. "But a wise tongue
will speak a healing word."

—Proverbs 12:18

"Oh, all you do is scold me!"
Susanna's lip stuck out.
"It makes me feel so creepy.
It makes me want to pout."

"I scold because I love you.
The really wise folk know
it's good to be corrected.
Correction helps us grow."
—*Proverbs 12:1*

"Let's talk about the heavens,"
said Susanna with a sigh.
"My cousin Dan says stars
are candy flowers in the sky."

Grandma laughed and laughed and laughed.
"How silly some folk are!
Wise ones stop and think before
they try to eat a star."
—*Proverbs 14:15*

"Well, even so, I'm hungry!"
Susanna ran inside
and came back with a plate of cakes.
"Now, Grandma, you decide . . .

“Rebecca has a little dog.
I wish that it were mine.
I asked my dad to get me one,
but he just said, ‘Don’t whine.’ ”

“A jealous heart can make you whine.
It makes you feel ill.
Love both Rebecca *and* her dog
and let your heart be still.”
—*Proverbs 14:30*

"Oh, Grandma!" cried Susanna.
"I want to be so *good.*
I want to do such *glorious* things.
Do you think I ever could?"

"Give all your plans to God, child.
Ask Him to make you strong.
Ask Him to bless each thing you do
and then you can't go wrong."
—*Proverbs 16:3*

Susanna jumped up from her seat
and hugged her grandma tight.
"I love you, Grandma, and I'm sure
you're always, always, right!"

"You're not so bad yourself, my child.
In fact, you are my crown.
The Book of Proverbs says that too.
And now I must lie down.
—Proverbs 17:6

"But here's the most important piece
of knowledge ever stored.
The first thing really wise folk do
is love and serve the Lord."
—*Proverbs 1:7*

DEAR PARENTS:

Most of us have grown up with proverbs—"Go to the ant, thou sluggard!" "Spare the rod . . ," etc. We treat them a lot like folk wisdom and quote them at appropriate moments. Scholarship seems to indicate, though, that the Biblical proverbs aren't a collection of folk wisdom at all, but rather the work of learned persons—persons like Solomon—written in poetic form to educate young people of the upper classes.

The way the proverbs do this is to describe what life is like. "When you give something away, you usually get even more back. That's how life is. If you want to grow in knowledge, you'd better be willing to take correction. Life's like that too."

These are important lessons that can mean as much to children—and adults—today as they did to people thousands of years ago. But there's one more thing your child should know, especially when he or she occasionally fails to live according to the proverbs. God forgives. He sent His Son to die for us and so when we mess up, we can ask for that forgiveness. We can have a fresh start—as many fresh starts as we need.

THE EDITOR